4:56

4:56
POEMS
CARLOS
FUENTES
LEMUS

EDITED BY E. SHASKAN BUMAS
AFTERWORD BY JUAN GOYTISOLO

DALKEY ARCHIVE PRESS
CHAMPAIGN
DUBLIN
LONDON

Library of Congress Cataloging-in-Publication Data

Fuentes Lemus, Carlos.
  4:56 : poems / Carlos Fuentes Lemus ; edited by E. Shaskan Bumas, with Alejandro Branger ;
introduction by E. Shaskan Bumas ; afterword by Juan Goytisolo. -- 1st ed.
    p. cm.
  Includes index.
  ISBN 978-1-56478-679-1 (pbk. : acid-free paper)
  I. Bumas, E. Shaskan, 1961- II. Branger, Alejandro. III. Title.
  PQ6706.U476A2 2012
  861'.7--dc23
                    2011041214

Portions of this book initially appeared in *the minnesota review*

The editor gratefully acknowledges the creative collaboration of his co-editor Alejandro Branger

Partially funded by a grant from the Illinois Arts Council, a state agency, and by the University
of Illinois at Urbana-Champaign

www.dalkeyarchive.com

Cover: design and composition by Danielle Dutton, painting by Carlos Fuentes Lemus
Printed on permanent/durable acid-free paper and bound in the United States of America

CONTENTS

INTRODUCTION

THE CARLOS FUENTES LEMUS EXPERIENCE

Like many kids who are encouraged to create, Carlos Fuentes Lemus wrote and drew from the time he could hold a pencil. When he was five, his teacher in New Jersey sent some of his pictures to Shankar's International Children's Competition, in New Delhi, but only mentioned the competition after he had won a prize. After that early success, Fuentes Lemus never stopped drawing. At ages six and seven, he sketched his family—instantly recognizable yet iconic—with sure and confident lines. He was gifted. Over the next few years, he became obsessed with the greats of art history. He memorized the life of Vincent Van Gogh, but, when he was thirteen, that wasn't enough. Enamored with the sunflowers in Van Gogh's paintings, Fuentes Lemus planted sunflower seeds in his garden in Cambridge, England, a town not famous for its sunshine. Several times a day, he stood above the seedlings with a watering can, impatient for something to paint. He left the flowers to fend for themselves during a family vacation, but on returning home they had grown taller than he was, and he was ready to paint them. Though other painters would be at least as influential on him, he thought of Van Gogh throughout his life, as evidenced by a line he wrote on May 5, 1999, the day of his death: "delirium does not deform a Van Gogh painting."

To be a child with a powerful imagination was to be in paradise, but because of the rules and limits that circumscribe children, this paradise, like others, was lost. Even fate took the form of rules and constraints: grown-ups telling kids what they couldn't do. And as Carlos Fuentes Lemus grew up, such grown-up constraints as the year and place he was born (1973, Paris, France), the country of his citizenship (Mexico), where he grew up (the U.S., mostly New Jersey), and his medical disorder (hemophilia) were all part of his fate, but he did his best to play with these constraints, these limits that otherwise seemed destined to define him. For Fuentes Lemus, freedom from fate was staked out by taking photos, painting, shooting film, and writing poems. Put another way, a source of Carlos Fuentes Lemus's inspiration became his ability to accept all the hard knocks of experience and still remain a child, and his poetics was to offer his experience to readers in the hope that they would kindle, or rekindle, the enthusiasm of their own childhoods.

Carlos Fuentes Lemus never lost faith in the creative genius he associated with children. His memories of childhood may strike a reader as Wordsworthian, but that's only accurate to a point. Whereas William Wordsworth would write "Intimations of Immortality from Recollections of Early Childhood," Fuentes Lemus picked up on intimations of *mortality* from recollections of early childhood. He died in 1999 at twenty-five, so it turns out he had very good reason to feel the weight of mortality. In their disparate voices, the first two poems of this collection—the first written at twenty-four, as a recollection of when he was five, and the latter written at thirteen—tell us that as a little boy, and thereafter, Carlos Fuentes Lemus was aware of, and accepted, the inevitability, even the ubiquity of death. At five, everything changes when he realizes that one day his parents will die. This insight is not unusual for a five-year-old—and that it is not unusual is part of the reason that Fuentes Lemus thought children were geniuses—but it is thought-provoking to contextualize this as an early epiphany. To remember and to heed this insight as an adult is an act of sustained courage. Exuberant at thirteen, he loved John Keats, who died at twenty-five, and to love Keats is to love beauty and the power of the imagination. Fuentes Lemus's early poem notes the presence of death, but presents himself flying "into the future," not as a disembodied spirit but as a young man with a body. If his earliest memories were about the inevitability of death, his earliest extant poems were about freedom and power and color, death in the context of having fun, of creating, of living.

Fuentes Lemus was a devourer of literature. When he was still barely big enough to carry them, he carted around fat biographies of Arthur Rimbaud (Starkie) and of Oscar Wilde (Ellman), two of his favorite writers, despite the great differences in their philosophies—though the former would have claimed interest in nothing less than the deepest soul, and the latter in nothing more than the most polished surfaces, both led lives on scales large enough to compete with their canonical works. Most of the writers he loved wrote in English, and this might seem strange when we think that he held a Mexican passport and that he was the son of a Spanish-language novelist. But Carlos Fuentes Lemus grew up in the U.S., schooled in Princeton, New Jersey; Hanover, New Hampshire; Saint Louis, Missouri; and Washington, DC; Boston and later Cambridge, Massachusetts; though also in Cambridge and later London, England; Normandy, France; and Mexico City, mostly near colleges where his father instructed. Though often at the top of his class, he never finished high school. Fuentes Lemus had popular tastes and loved many aspects of U.S. popular culture: rock music, movies, poetry. Still, for him, and for his sister Natasha Fuentes, who by virtue of being born here had a U.S. passport—and Mexican parents—nationality was fungible. They were very bright young people, and very polite, even diplomatic.

I knew Carlos Fuentes Lemus since he was eight because his father was one of my college professors. When their family passed through New York, and I was working there, I took Carlos and Natasha around Manhattan on the subway. In November, 1987, Natasha was content to buy a pair of checked Vans to take back to her French boarding school. Carlos towed us all around town (as he usually did with me when I was allegedly his guide) to shop for photos of his favorite movie stars (James Dean) and records of his favorite music (Elvis Presley). He was shorter than average, and if his photo was taken, he might stand on his toes to be taller than his kid sister. That day, a middle-aged and well-informed Tower Records salesman kept changing subjects from one musical genre another, from opera to gospel, from music to movies, from movies to books, and thirteen- and fourteen-year-old Natasha and Carlos, who had access to all this and more in their artistic household, followed every nuance and discussed every subject of interest to him with keen intelligence.

The man, a little stunned, took a step back, glanced at me for encouragement or explanation, then asked the young people, perhaps because of their slight, unplaceable accents, "Where are you from?"

"Mexico," they said as one.

The acceptance of the presence of death in life is more often considered a part of Mexican culture than of U.S. culture (according to the early work of Elisabeth Kübler-Ross on the former and the novels of the father Carlos Fuentes on the latter). And while Fuentes Lemus was a Mexican citizen, he was basically a United States of American kid, so it's more likely his health than his nationality that made him one of the few people in the US not in need of a *memento mori*. Fuentes Lemus had hemophilia, which meant that he couldn't produce blood plasma with the clotting agent called Factor VIII. Hemophilia was long a famous disease because Queen Victoria of England was a carrier, and most of her children suffered from the condition. Its reputation was queered when Victoria's great-grandson Alexei was born with hemophilia, which led to his mother, Alexandra, falling under the influence of the Russian mystic Rasputin. Russians called it "the English disease." From 1840, hemophilia was treated with blood infusions, but from the mid-1960s, thanks to the discoveries of Dr. Judith Graham Pool, hemophiliacs could be treated with collected Factor VIII concentrated by freezing blood plasma. Rasputins were no longer necessary. Because the seats at the hospital were made for grown-ups, as a toddler, Carlos Fuentes Lemus, had to sit in his mother's lap to receive an injection of Factor VIII. He cried. On the way home, his mother, Silvia Lemus, told him that he would need these injections forever and that he was being brave. The next time he was back at the hospital, after some of the roughhousing three-year-olds crave, he rolled up his own sleeve for the injection and he did not cry.

A few years later things became worse for hemophiliacs. In 1981, the Center for Disease Control reported a particular sarcoma affecting gay men and later affecting intravenous drug users. By 1982, when Carlos Fuentes Lemus was eight, the CDC linked the disease to human blood. Still, at least one company continued recruiting blood donors from at-risk populations. Soon there were hemophilia patients who developed the disease. Later that year, when Fuentes Lemus was nine, the disease was renamed AIDS. A year later, French researchers found the virus HIV. By 1983 there was a method to clean the plasma used for Factor VIII. However, Cutter Laboratories, an affiliate of Bayer, continued selling Factor VIII that had already been manufactured, and manufactured more for sale in certain countries without employing the new safety measures. Despite righteous haranguing from Surgeon General C. Evert Koop, the federal government invested little in research of, or in education about, AIDS. By 1985, the Food and Drug Administration had approved a test for HIV. In 1985, responding to a reporter's question, President Ronald Reagan made his first public mention of the disease, and two years later gave his first speech on the epidemic. 1985 is also when blood *products* such as Factor VIII were first tested. By this time, half of the people in the United States with hemophilia were infected with HIV. Carlos Fuentes Lemus was one of them. Good treatment for HIV and AIDS came out in 1994, and by 1995 there was the first protease inhibitor. 1996 saw the first AIDS cocktails of medicines to include antiretroviral formulas.

Carlos Fuentes Lemus lived his life during these times of slow progress and victim blaming, and he went on practicing his various arts: at first his painting and poetry, later photography. There were also advantages to being Carlos Fuentes Lemus. He was doted on by his family, perhaps as much as any son and brother has ever been doted on. He could afford, with health insurance, Factor VIII, advanced medicine, and consultations with talented Mexican physicians. He had a life of travel among famous, accomplished people: movie director Luis Buñuel, who gave him a baby bath; novelist Gabriel García Márquez, whom he could ask for advice during a rough patch; William Styron, who put him up in Martha's Vineyard; and novelist Juan Goytisolo, who read his poems. Fuentes Lemus got his first Leica camera in his early teens. As he went around with his parents to visit relatives and friends, mostly from the art world, but also the occasional politician, he might sit on the floor, inconspicuous by virtue of looking younger than his young age, and wield a small range-finder camera that might or might not have been loaded with film. These photos are all about feeling and context; they are composed, but not formal. Few of them are sharply focused. They are very grainy. His first published photo, of his father and Salman Rushdie in London, appeared in Madrid's *El País* a few days after the *fatwah* of 1989. Along with written portraits by his father, many of his photos were published in 1998 in the Spanish-reading world in a collection called *Retratos en el tiempo* (Portraits in Time). The pictures, all taken in Fuentes Lemus's teens, are "in time" in the sense that time is depicted, captured, with no attempt to render his often famous subjects with the usual glossiness, or severed from their actual contexts: Gabriel García Márquez talks with his hands; classic ranchera singer Lola Beltrán is emotionally moved in a clump of people at a party (including, judging from the glimpse of a sport jacket, García Márquez again); writer Susan Sontag has a smoke while staring at her son, David Rieff, who seems to have, thanks to a trick perspective, his mother's head balanced on his hand; economist John Kenneth Galbraith looms extra-long in an extra-large bathrobe; singer-songwriter Carly Simon laughs with Jacqueline Kennedy Onassis; Gregory Peck blends into the desert and the sky on the set of *Old Gringo*; actress Audrey Hepburn turns to bid good-bye and disappear into the night. The book sold, in the Mexican idiom, like fresh-baked bread.

Fuentes Lemus also loved the sensibilities of the Beats: the spontaneity of Allen Ginsberg's "first thought, best thought"; William S. Burroughs's highlighting of marginal people and making them cool; the image of the roll of paper on which Jack Kerouac wrote *On the Road* without stopping, save to take more speed. Carlos Fuentes Lemus took Kerouac's title as a commandment. In 1989, when he was just shy of his sixteenth birthday, I drove him on his first annual trip to Memphis and Tupelo. This was a pilgrimage to Graceland and the stations of Elvis's Southern life, always on August 16, the anniversary of Elvis's death. It was also a chance for Fuentes Lemus to take pictures of people who shared his enthusiasm, and likewise to take pictures of their relics—in a sense, pictures of the absence of Elvis. Fuentes Lemus was shy and used the camera in part as a mask to conceal himself, when he might have been participating in the Elvis festivities—though he wanted to. The Elvis pilgrimage became an annual ritual for him and his friends. The road widened and became a subject of his poetry and film, such as when the road took him to the Ashford Motel, where, as he observes in the poem that begins "Burn victims," "The tv's gonna explode." The road eventually included the sky, and the poem "Nubia bye-bye" tells of a prostitute he met in Cartagena, Colombia, "a too good person," during the 1994 film festival, by which time he had stopped shooting stills with the Leica.

In a sense the photos were a respite from painting. In 1986 and '87, Fuentes Lemus made stunning self-portraits, in many of which the color yellow figured prominently. Some of these portraits were funny: Over a pencil sketch, he added white paint to his face, and depicted his hay fever with blotches of red on his throat, nose, ears, and in and around his eyes. A portrait of Morrissey, with a yellow background, combines the face of the singer with that of the painter. These pictures are bright and vibrant and gorgeous. When I asked him about his painting, however, a couple of years later, on our trip to Memphis and Tupelo, he said he'd stopped, because his paintings were looking too much like Egon Schiele's. They did look like Schiele's, but they were luminous.

Fuentes Lemus returned to painting in New York in the early 1990s, and soon thereafter to poetry. He had a whole new painting style, inspired by Jean-Michel Basquiat. He painted on cardboard in thick gobs of fleshy abstraction with figurative iconography (often a mother and child or scenes from the life of Elvis) scattered purposely throughout. This was a style that would serve him well when his health, including his vision, took turns for the worse. This was also the most productive time of Fuentes Lemus's life as a poet. He had replaced Keats with the Beats in a decisive manner. He and his sister lived with their friend Alejandro Branger, a Venezuelan-US dual citizen, who was pursuing a BA in film at NYU, and they all worked on his student movies together: Natasha Fuentes in front of the camera and her brother behind, working on the crew. Fuentes Lemus served as on-set still photographer as well, writing poems about having to deal with the inevitable hoodlums encountered while making a movie on the streets of New York, and learning the film trade in the process. They frequented the Pyramid and Smalls Jazz Club. Brother and sister hung out at the Chelsea Hotel where they met the poet Herbert Huncke, a Beat icon. These were heedless times for Carlos and Natasha and their friends in New York. On one representative occasion, returning home after a long all-nighter, having forgotten their keys or because someone inside was too zonked to open up, Fuentes Lemus's cousin rappelled down the apartment building's wall, carrying a crowbar that he used to pry open a window—though, alas, the window was to someone else's apartment. This was the ecstatic of crazed young people, the exuberance of close calls, the experience and experimentation they believed would inform their art, and was more reckless than feckless.

In 1994, Fuentes Lemus started shooting his own movie, at points titled *Lay Lady Lay* after Dylan, whom he idealized for marrying rock and the Beats; then *One for My Baby*, as in the Johnny Mercer and Harold Arlen song made famous by Sinatra, which continues, "and one more for the road"; and eventually *Gallo de Pelea*, a title that is bilingual in a personal manner because the Spanish means "Fighting Cock" and his protagonist was, in English, "cocky." The motion picture camera replaced his Leica. Many of the scenes are based on Fuentes Lemus's poems and their aesthetic seems less narrative than descriptive. There is also a road-trip element to the plot, starting from Providence, Rhode Island, where a Neal Cassady sort of character, Phil, has to flee after a fight (as did the actor, now artist and provocateur, Duke Riley) and winds up in Mexico after various picaresque adventures, only to flee again after committing more violence. The character stops to visit the lead actor's uncle and then Fuentes Lemus's uncle in turn, to chew the fat. Then Phil goes to Cerro del Quemado in San Luís Potosí, original home of the Huichol (Wixáritari) people and to where the Huichol return annually for ritual peyote ceremonies. The crew had, and filmed, their own desert ceremonies. When Phil goes into town, he has an idyllic relationship with a prostitute (played by Natasha Fuentes): a second chance, which soon enough is blown.

Liam Davis, Fuentes Lemus's friend from high school, and Liam's brother, Tim, both worked on the shoot. Liam interprets the movie as a loose type of "allegory," concerning Fuentes Lemus's HIV and his desire to reform, though he insists that this is just his interpretation. *Gallo de Pelea* resists analysis. The film was never finished, in part because some of the film wasn't coded, so the picture and sound couldn't be synchronized, and in part because other portions of the soundtrack were lost. Fuentes Lemus worked on and fretted about the film for the rest of his life, even as his health worsened.

In 1996, Carlos Fuentes Lemus came down with meningitis, which was complicated by HIV, hemophilia, uneven medical attention, imperfect water, and the exuberant style of life fed by a feeling of invincibility natural to most men in their twenties, in this case multiplied by the number of times he had already survived such crises against all odds. He went into a coma from which he unexpectedly came out, alive but scathed: having lost some vision and the ability to move easily. He dropped to around ninety pounds. Thereafter he was never again completely well: unable to see, to digest food, or to walk about as well as he had before. His vision was, in his own description, "pixelated," broken into bits like the magnified image of a television screen. When feeling gradually returned to parts of his body, he felt little beyond pain. With shaky hand he struggled to write the thirty-word poem "Texass / Texis." It is a tour de force of condensed meaning. In it, Fuentes Lemus thinks about what it means, as a United States of American guy with Mexican citizenship, to be in Texas, the first of several states to be transferred from Mexico to the U.S., after a tasteful period of independence: a slave state. It was pronounced *Texis*, but spelled more like *Tex-ass*. The ass, after all, is a common synecdoche for an entire person, as in, get your *ass* over here. An unattributed question lingers: "Is your ass Tex or Mex?" This could also pose another question of identity: "Is you' Aztecs or Mex?" Given the state of his health and vision, given his prognosis, Fuentes Lemus wonders if it makes any difference whether he's Tex or Mex. He can no longer feel his ass, his self. From the hospital window he seems to see nightingales pecking on crackers, but the *crackers* may just be white people, or the crackers might be (he wouldn't feel it) his own ass. Because nightingales have never settled in the States, with his blurred vision, Fuentes Lemus is seeing the world through his first master of poetry, the exquisite John Keats, constructing a world in which a thing of beauty—here as André Breton insisted, a convulsive beauty—is a joy forever.

Fuentes Lemus wrote lyric poetry in English, but where necessary uses some Spanish. "The *ganas* left me," he begins a poem, in a low mood, which is like saying that his *desires*, or *wants*, have disappeared, not in a Buddhist sense of the desire to be rid of desire, but in the sense of bottoming out. Even English has let him down, and so a more Spanish syntax takes over in the next lines, affirming the meaning of the first: "for my world / this life." We are put in mind of Rilke's "Torso of an Archaic Apollo," which tells us to change our lives. Ending the poem with an ambiguous "I want," the poet betrays that he will find it harder to change his life than to change his syntax. In another alternation of English and Spanish, a belligerent poem from San Luís Potosí, he writes in musical end-stopped lines:

> What if we built a golf course on virgin land
> Ride your donkey to the green
> Tee off under the Huichol sol
> Land your ball in the Virgen's mouth
> And never again have to pray for pain and rain

The idea of virgin land, ripe for development, is recognizable from the historiography of what is called American Studies, where the land and nature were female, and the indigenous people were part of nature. In this poem, the *locus amoenus* has been repurposed as a golf course, and old US discourses of eminent domain, that microcosm of Manifest Destiny, are imported. *Virgen* is spelled in Spanish, because the word refers to the Virgin of Guadalupe who appeared to the native Juan Diego soon after the Spanish Conquest, and who was very helpful when Juan tried to prove her presence to the church fathers and to convince them to build, not a golf course, but a church, where she had appeared and performed miracles.

In the long poem that begins "Imagined hats are tipped," there are other uses of a personal Spanglish: if "Hunger . . . dures longer than Mañana," this malnutrition will last a good long while. The vocabulary recalls Dylan's "A Hard Rain's a-Gonna Fall." *Dures* is a Spanish word conjugated in English, like our *duration,* and pronounced like Jim Morrison's band. Before a reader can come to some conclusion here about Spanglish as an emblem of identity, Fuentes Lemus lists Javanese flora and fauna in Latin and cites what sounds like tourist Indonesian, except when it becomes more like Indonenglish. Spanish appears when a Spanish word is the best way to say something, and often the Spanish isn't exactly Spanish yet is more exact for just that reason. When the sum of English and Spanish, and perhaps language itself, could not express his physical pain, Fuentes Lemus returned to his paints: to cover a piece of cardboard in thick globs of black with red and white, to glue on gauze and other medical supplies and pictures from magazines, and then to inscribe in it his personal iconography of mother and child and Elvis's progress through life. He put the pain in his paints. In the poems, his mask was his voice. These poems are prayers of observation.

In one, a literal transition into Spanish of the English phrase "to make love" becomes something of a disquisition on the creation of love and the difficulties of intimacy when one's lover is HIV positive:

> I used to laugh when you said
> "hacer el amor." Love makes itself.
> Love dovetails. I believed my
> own guilt. The universe's condemnation.
> But it's cool with the condom

People with HIV were never condemned by the universe, I hardly need to point out, just by people who thought that god was as big a bigot as they were. In the absence of AIDS education in the 1980s, paranoia reigned and in some places children with HIV were banned from schools, or even—in the case of a Florida family with three hemophiliac HIV-positive sons—run out of town. AIDS often flared from the background of the foreground of public discourse, in confused and panicked images on TV and in the tabloids that occupied living rooms and waiting rooms and bedrooms and empty rooms. Under such circumstances, it would be difficult for a young man to keep out the idea that his condition was some sort of metaphor for his being, and to believe that he wasn't being punished for something with these terrible diseases. When you're being blamed by others for your own suffering, it is hard not to blame yourself. Carlos Fuentes Lemus dealt with the repercussions of his disease in his poetry by testing its limits, by leading with the condom. This casual alliterative passage vanquishes that wicked metaphor.

No poet is an island of discourse. Aside from invective, there are earwigs. Snatches of songs pop into Carlos Fuentes Lemus's poems as they might into anyone's head at any time. After the "Hard Rain" of "Imagined hats," there's part of a line from Dylan's "Like a Rolling Stone." The discourse of "Bob Dylan said" takes up where Dylan's song "Dignity" ends. And Elvis is everywhere: even in these poems. Fuentes Lemus feints in one poem toward "Hound Dog," but stays with the less canonical Elvis: "Old Shep," which is *actually* about a dog, "I'll Hold You in My Arms," and "Harbor Lights." He starts off another poem with a line that also begins a song by the Jimi Hendrix Experience, "I Don't Live To-day": "Will I live tomorrow." Whereas Hendrix, at twenty-four, makes the soulful pronouncement that he's not alive now, Fuentes Lemus, at twenty-four, insists that he "ain't going away." This is the Carlos Fuentes Lemus experience. Aside from those of rockers, the "song" with the most influence on these poems was "The Ballad of Reading Gaol," the moving story of an execution by Oscar Wilde, writing under the pen name C.C.3, that is, the designation of his cell in the eponymous jail at the same time that the execution took place. Fuentes Lemus plays with the refrain: "Each man kills the thing he loves." He was haunted by that Wilde line whenever he and the one (or "the thing") he loved put their faith, and his cock, in a latex tube. This is where the ideal of childhood genius can do no more for him. When children grow up, they must recognize that others have a subjectivity such as they had only granted to themselves: "'cause what / am I but an underweight, paranoid / egomaniac. You got your own worries." Now freedom will come from getting beyond the limits of the self, from empathy. For Carlos Fuentes Lemus, the "thing" he loves becomes one person. At the end of his life, the person was Yvette Fuentes (no relation), with whom, her young son Alfredo along for the trip, he spent his last day, and who, according to what he wrote on that last day, was the one to remind him that things don't and people don't and relationships don't last forever. In his first extant poem, death was manifest, and on the day that his heart stopped pumping blood, he wrote that his girlfriend reminded him they wouldn't be around forever.

The image of freedom for Carlos Fuentes Lemus was the child who thinks through exploration and play, but that freedom was threatened by a fate embodied by grown-ups who "make children do everything against their nature." The trick was to continue childhood spontaneity in harshest adulthood. He always believed this. At seven, Fuentes Lemus wrote a story in his Hanover school about a newborn fifty-year-old man who becomes younger with every passing birthday. Forty-seven birthdays later, the three-year old is riding a new tricycle when he dies of a heart attack and goes to heaven. Fuentes Lemus still admires, in the poem that starts "All these solitary pages," the childishness of an eighty-year-old man putting jelly beans in people's shoes. And so he invented a way that his readers could be childlike. There is a game like "I Spy with My Little Eye" in his poems: we spy Oscar and Vincent, Dylan, Elvis, Howlin' Wolf, and Hendrix in poems of love and despair, of humiliation and power, poems that might turn out to be as grave as the renunciation of life. These are very serious games. Despite the physical pain he experienced, Fuentes Lemus took pleasure in language, as in rhyme: "rent on the tent"; "Your social skills / are social ills." The rhyming is childlike, but not childish in a Dr. Seuss sense. It's play. It's fun. It can make us think of life in a different way. The play is necessary, and the poet has ambition: "If I could get / out what I feel / for everyone, it would / be a violent Love. / I would crack ribs / bite off lips / swallow tongues / and scratch my name / across your heart." The poet gets out a remarkable amount of how he feels. And if a poem begins "Who invited me to Hell?" and ends by rhyming *terrace, furnace, burn us,* and *Circus,* then you don't have to be John Milton (or his Satan) to find that in his hell, Fuentes Lemus is constructing heaven.

E. SHASKAN BUMAS, 2012

4:56

There was a hollow
In the brain waiting
to be filled
excavated to return
to childhood vision.
Wake up use your
toilet bowl Jacuzzi,
your varnished castle,
with hand size enemies
swallow butterflies.
You sleep in a quilted field
with other people your size
covered in hair and
licking between their legs.
Are those two double your
head size bony, jointed
pieces crushing or caressing?
The hairy beast that tries
to touch your delicatessen.
Your pink flesh. It spills out
For you. But how he
gives more happiness than you.
Her hand that gets away
my itch. That gets me apples
to my teeth. No, they can't

play in gardens as big as mine.
They eat tiny bananas. Their bodies
are always crunched. A dive from
boards ten times higher than them.
Ha! They have to do things they
hate. They're all scared of each other.
But one day we will all be gone
my parents will be gone.
It's dark green and I cry.

May 1998
memory of being 5

THE HEART OF THE SPARROW

Through white cotton puffs
In the blue satin sky
My metal winged sparrow;
With me in its eye,
Roars over long ribbons of green
Large patch work quilts comfort the soil.

My heart to the sky,
Soul to the heavens
Love to the gods
Sins to the ashes
To myself the heart of the sparrow.

Family away, civilization below.
Pathway of stone, lead me
Indulge me sharp beak
For you put in this blue:
A naive young man.

Thoughts of death gleam in my eye
But there is no reason why
For land locked I shall soon be.

No more rays of orange sun
Or streaks of reddening white

They all shall glide into the past,
I shall land into the future.

October 16, 1986

1

Greased feet and tin can jaw
a large black smile and circled eyes
      the horse's head
            green wooden teeth
            the big bald blue skull
            make children do everything
                  against their nature

2

Like a young cat'll
      jump five feet
      in the air to catch a butterfly
      and eat it
      a terrorist bomb'll blow
you out of the sky

Milkiness and diamonds
boyvisions through Harlem
sea of slurs
punch and beatin' up a jukebox
granite karmas
85 cent sandwiches
it's the last fair deal goin' down
from Vicksburg poisin wiskee
rubbin' a black chick's belly
gauzed over with a name
ran across the street in
baggy pants
open your eyes wide
when a bus pass by
and remember blue tinted
windows of a Mexican
landscape
and your heavenly wristwatch

June 1993

1

I can't be seen
doing something
emotional. Sex
yes. <u>Don't</u> see
me write. But
I won't hide
in the bathroom.
Too much of
the same.
Who has to ask
for

2

Protection?
Can't share pain
and the joy
in reuniting
with the lost?
You're coming,
I'll go,
I'll be
Silent.

February 1999

All these solitary pages,
they need comfort & caress.
Otherwise they cannot return
their companionship & grip
on this world and yourself.
Your inner self. What dies when
one becomes an adult? When you've
grown as child yelled at to stop
asking questions. Who mistreats
Children, theirs or others. Only
Children and Animals should populate.
Nothing is done by them to leave their Place
in history. Or there is cynicism,
flipness. Even an 80-year-old man,
a respected and respect-demanding man
will put jelly beans in your shoes
while you sleep. Smirk through the
streets, look at sky free, alone creating
one energy from the other great Energy.
In the subway with ricocheting
moods & vibes & quick glances and
trying to ignore. Seeing who
you could trust and who'll fear you.

Softness in secrecy.
The woman that makes you

forget the world around. No matter
Looks, clothing. Not superficial, maybe
you notice but don't care 'cause what
am I but an underweight, paranoid
egomaniac. You got your own worries.

You gotta measure the confession.
Which can be so casual, except when
Man made germs destroy two humans'
natural, easy comfort & ease. dis & dis.

December 1997

Imagined hats are tipped
A truly misunderstanding.
What Renaissance Prince?
Court & all.
People impressed, kinder,
'cause of one fact?
"a fantastic collection of
stamps" (etc.) ?
Junk dealers with complete
library of Expressionist painters.
Track mark & bone hookers
being picky about their
salmon & onion bagels, she
was once great at roller
disco,
And the Hawaiian surf
champ, nose and boob jobbed,
wanting me to place my
foot in her bare crotch
(my socked foot) to calm
her crack horniness
While she, as Mata Hari
has evil farces trying
to make her go to the convent.
Not undercover.

She'd be under wraps.
No more exclusive
rights to forgotten Hitchcock
films. Her blood-shitting,
moonshine-drinking husband just
stopped at the bar
of Rehabilitation just
outside the framed Pictures
of his jet and hard-on.
Crashing. Under waves
of Coked-out Clichés.
Briefly the Pelican.
Then the licking of
Giacometti, Polska, Fujeira
and a fair weather haired
Beethoven.

The Emperor's chosen
Ink Man lay for ten
years before drafting
the perfect Crab in
Ten seconds. 20. 30.
Push to 90. The Queen
isn't stamped-on
unlike the Brushtail Possum,
The Australian who
made Von Something's
                    Yacht

The Crab opened
and by flew the Penerbangan
Pertama Insgris into
the jaws of Redubuk
Pariwisata.

They cackle at the
unknown future political
terrorist. No more funny
Thai dancers. Pop is not
happy at Boom Doom.
Rightly reveling in his
Rebelling: which is just
dropping self-righteousness.
Roll your dice into
the Volcano. One dog's
head peers from the lava
while the Popo sings
"Old Shep" and 8 cents
will get your words
across the world, where
Hunger is gold framed
and dures longer than
Mañana, stepping bare foot on
every variety of pebbles,
cockles & shells, eating
Ornithoptera chimaera,
Sagra speciosa and

sometimes Dendrobium brac-
teosum.

"('Rebirth; A renaissance
Prince must die where,
When & how he chooses.'
(minus suicide))"

Of Natural cause like
the scorpion who was
just drowned in a bottle
of Mezcal. And you
can't be afraid to drink
me.

August 1997

Poplar Ave
        big tit at end of
        the road
        or leaving it

In Paris the clouds lift
He sees the pretty joy
of a new place
and finds absinthe.

A worker in his
spiritual soil
bends with the wind
as one bird flaps its
wings.

He starts to break
down the city &
        culture he's in
Paints golden apples
that everyone should
        be able to eat.

Monsieur Van Gogh
brother Vincent
formed by one background

which he reshapes & recolors
The divisions of
country & city

you can feel the breeze
see the pollen sparkle
on a winding road
without your couple.
            without your love

The crunch & the
wind of the hard
grain. The Yellow
that protects from rain

The landscape you
put your signature on
            the small town
            Pyramid.

It's a day you want
to walk through
            again

            clear divisions
of earth & sky

You pulled off
your comfort.

You pulled on your sheets
You want your internal
Fragments of the sun,
          chunks of sun
& real Fragments of
the stars and
sweet cave man chair

churned earth Makes
the clear sky rugged

clouds are tossed by
waves at the dead
          boat sea
parked in Mackerel sand

          The Zouave is
          sad drunk but
          perceptive

          Yellow Fever.
          It does look like
a marvelous world that
          needs retelling

The garden at the
Hospital is rougher than
the streaked sky

the baby's limbs
under blossom branches

The single butterfly
takes to the skully leaves
& poppies

There's something actually
soft about the pink
roses, an old woman's
powdered skin

The total sea
of organic shit growth
on bended trees
In a car window
blur

It's the best place
to rest wish it
to never go away

but imagine it
burnt & frozen
in ash.

Never been a better
understanding of
magic hour

of perfect
          spirit time
that everyone deserves

The clear dry
Earthen pale image
of death

The wheat field
full of invisible mothers

And a true pale
green southern sky

neon ravines
& olive groves
with lion hearts

Jesus is taken away
by cobalt electricity
drained & then recharged
Man in a park
with fallen Leaves
crumbling cottages
drooping grass
                    graying landscape
                    Flat mountain
                         Clouds

Amsterdam, October 1994

Faded Dryness of patio snails
Lizards do pushups hump on wall
Butterfly flowers try for their freedom
Flying in place petrified
Like under water wood of millions

Cacti dare you to join their orgies
That guy's not Jesus, he's just walking his goats

What if we built a golf course on virgin land
Ride your donkey to the green
Tee off under the Huichol sol
Land your ball in the Virgen's mouth
And never again have to pray for pain and rain

The rain and the pain
The rain and the hail
The train and the nail
The rain just pulled into town
Have visions of the churches
Crumbling into each other
The blues tone
Blue stones of Cathedrals
Crashing into each other like
Holy hail stones

March 2, 1994

Air brought to life by
crackling rumba
Everything is made red
by red whore lighting

Silver-speckled drinking tables
covered by interlocking liquid glass rings
Their silver lacquered
nails twirl swizzle sticks
in cubas since beginningless time

She looks like the love of your life
Love of her night
of slapping skins
of towel wiping
Her baby-oiled nights
don't think that you're funny

There's always
been wind and speed
to blow your face free
In Lowell Massachusetts
you get suspicious looks
just as human as
anyone
peeling blue paint
and bikers pulling
their pants down
soaking a dry skull
in whiskey
curious kids
Black and Latin led
by white women

where they want
people as a person
and no cheap sympathies
in symphonies
of frying potatoes

1993

John Smith
Old Jazz Man
Walk like
Inhales like
Smile at women like
Shake your hand like
Take a bus like
Hear thru the
Walls and floor like
He talks with
He picks up with
He cross the street in Atlanta
Georgia like
He eat Jazz
Don't sleep thru jazz
Sleep in jazz
Remembers in jazz
He plays his life
Kew KEW ARE
es tee tee
You Vee Dubble you
-Ex-Why Z?

Burn victims
angry black women
rhinestone sunglasses
with bus drivers
chains and
tattooed foreheads
sooner or later
The tv's gonna explode
at the blind woman
cherry mouthed
future pimps
lock breakers
with faded green
metal suitcases
and no signs
of Pixie Dust

what it does it opens
up my aesophagus
brushcut father
of retarded boy
slamming bags
black plaster faced
whistles and don't forget

Was that a
scarecrow sign
or a man turned
into a why?
raisin his arms
in too tight overalls
and bulging seat belts
My Way
in shadows of street
lamps in 4 PM sun
Eex LSD FBI
Lovermont
Finger horns
Left up Right
PicnicTruckRest

Ashford Motel
off highway
behind trees.
You have just
passed
Ashford Motel

1993

My thoughts are the speed of
Clouds through the six sections
of the window the graphs of the
stacked buildings where lives mirror
each other where the same fast food
shit flows into the same water
a child's death you don't even want
to Imagine Where suspicious
mothers look at their kids
Where black men have real hate of
White men because of powers
Where a look can mean life,
between the eyes and
you imagine whatever in your
hand is liquor pulling your
eyes down to expose and see
yourself better to peel away
your hate to scrape off
your impurities to use
your tolls to get to know your family
try to make definite statements
Watch over your brother hearing voices
Watch everyone else and
just stare at the carpet
to easily hate what you're not part of
and love the ones who feel like you.

girls that make quesadillas
women that scream for their epazote
girls with doll legs
dough-filled faces
their patent shoes reflecting
who watch their real life soaps
who know that they're elegant
more than the street
who're proud of their families
who I don't know how they watch me
songs and visions

1993

Yesterdays mean nothin'
to him his guns on the ground.
My uncle workless, drinking brandy, existing,
doing little dances. Thinks the lonely one
ridiculous. But it's only 1962. He under-
stands. Drank moonshine Memphis '58. Liked
girl with tits like oranges. Flies drop dead
into the Jack Daniels then come out alive.
Start buzzing into God's ears,
who's sleeping, just a juggler with
greasy fingers.

1993

THE CREATION OF A NEW NEON UNIVERSE

A man in space
on a bicycle, smiling.
Every spoke on his chain
is a planet churning
at his will.

Carnival Neon planets
non stop Motion
on freefall roller coasters
Vegas Ferris-wheel lands.

Locomotive with a shiny Black man's face
pulling cots with coke snorting
plastic surgery babies.

1

Steel jawed spike
Toothed nuclear tipped
Tits of comic bomb

2

The flat-faced devil
Dog and silicone
Elephant fight it out
In city streets. Falling
Electric lines electrocute
Babies left in strollers
By fleeing parents

3

Under water looking
up at thundering
horses, ridden
by desperate men

4

Wildly painted
Men on highway
Dry town strip
(cops in back

arresting someone)
Stick their tongues
Up the moon

A cactus spinning
In a
GASETERIA
Man loses his
Shoes
The cash registers
Got the used
Car blues
And molded
Horses stampede
Into coal train

5
Layers of skin
Are eaten away
In dirt ground
Potato head
Dinosaur woman
in blond wig
Meets her lithograph
Face son

Goof off city-faced
Boy takes postcards to

Mother city of tour
To restaurant owned
By Crab on Alligator
In yellow sheets

In hill top home
Skeleton chested
Strippers pass you
By ceramic sculptures
Are crying to
Their mothers

Pink waterfall
Dissolve into
Flock of birds
Measuring the size
Of their skulls
Ghost of the family
In their home hallway
Father covered in shit
Sister becomes X-Ray flash
Mother is spouting
Son who is choking
Buried in muddy
Closet

6
A little girl in her
Dress is about

To be seduced by
A woman in a
Gray leather mask

Her gorilla saves
Her sends her
To life behind
A crack in the wall

7

A pinched-face
       Clown
Is smoking
Through his nose
'Cause he knows
He ain't got a mouth

8

And girls all over the
World were spelling
ELVIS in their Alpha-Bit
Soup except the
Blind girls who spelled
          VEILS

November 1992

Like a woman who can make a
deaf man hear, she can penetrate
your subconscious. One fingertip
touch instead of a million *shoot
that cum for me baby*s.
Though one of my erotic moments
was with a prostitute, it was the first
time dialogue was so important,
who took over her younger friend's
purely physical system <u>and</u> speaking,
called me a Malin in French, did
the job. I hate most people
with my characteristics. Fall in love
so easily, but don't understand
how any stranger, non familial
could love me?
I do want to know how many
arms have held you and why I
feel that mine understand you most.
Though you <u>are</u> the most erotic love
I used to laugh when you said
"hacer el amor." Love makes itself.
Love dovetails. I believed my
own guilt. The universe's condemnation.
But it's cool with the condom

'cause now it's all in the head.
It has been a dream with you.
<u>a dream</u>

August 1998

My obligatory 4:56 A.M.
discipline poem.

When how many times can
I say or think or write
that your skin is sex.
That we should spend
the rest of our lives,
eternity in this room
in the bed without coke
or booze.

You want me back and
your directness, not well
planned, but spontaneous,
criticizes me because
your eyes should see
another, but 8 months
24 hours a day
have given us ammunition.

September 1998

Thick sketched lips
On scratched in film face
Of rectangle headed
Woman with orange
Mist spirit
Body walking toward
Your flashlight hands
Reach for you. Ice
cream eyes look into
Each other her Cyclops
Tattoo winks in
Sunlight

1

staring at the ceiling
in Hotel Plaza
people make scientific studies
of the sheets
and last night I looked at
my face in the mirror for 3 hours
and saw it's not so evil

from one side of the air conditioner
        bugs crawl
on the right the sweating curtains
blind but hear scraping ice
        horns, sweeping
        cross street yells
        and shared mangoes

the girl with dark brown nipples
wears on a chain around her neck
jesus and the grim reaper
and she was even more beautiful
 in the black

and her rounded thighs walk
　her to a taxi

Tampico
June 5, 1993
The beginning of the rest of the end

　　　　2
a holy cross like a woman bending over
watches over
a sea lost in storm
on canvas
reflected in sticker mirror
a ripped '50s sofa
the floor looks like
they dig for oil
a wiry wax match
　　　its head crumbled
next to pena pura
this goes back to Providence
and hearing carnival music
el sol mio
　　　from a radio on a bandstand

Ware Ware MeCiEcho
pero el maya
masivo
and with eyes closed
those people are right
outside your window
pain smashed
like a holy cross
two girls
high in a
peach tree
a girl
over a
panther
always

1993

nubia bye bye
till tomorrow morning sight
of a too good person
with might to lean and scream
and dream of screens
and scram the lamb
and scramble the egg and beg
and scramble the bed and head
to the narrow halls of
the casanova hotel
her new home hot as hell

long street
white walls and a single tv
          frizz hair heat
king kong belts of pearls

and bottles of pearls
in unfurled neatness

blanking relations
eat your meatness
unsmiling then say it's loving
and we could if we would
and it was good with no hood

in a fusion of illusion
past life institutions

Who invited me to Hell?
Who invented me to tell
that the rent on the tent
has been spent on a dent
on the gates of Infernus?
Who tells me that the sad is rain,
that the black is train,
that the eye is face,
that I am a race,
that tonight is open,
that used are you, abused and headed
to use your affliction in the wrong direction
that your cure is to brew
the few that screw
'pon the terrace
hot as a furnace
always try burn us?
Barnum and Circus

A Look, Looking for a contact down at
Ruby's Downer Bar serve hot coffee on your face
Looking for a girl with a burnt face
in spurned lace, tights heights unknown
The player looks over, smiles
Her burnt face skipping drunk

Tied to a boomerang to a doom
See day under black rim of hat
Your day tinted bottle green
Your amber bottle face
Your broken bottle walk

Head on a heap of mattress
Mixed couple screw through wall
Says Fuck You on Papal paper
Coming through your ink
Interior wistful wishful filled
Enter you, Inter you
Hand over gun your rye
Down your over hung throat

February 1993

I'm gonna walk
them golden stairs,
not climb them.
Your social skills
are social ills.
Candle dripping
over elephants
remember this
night. When it
started 3 weeks ago.
You were falling
out of love.
into falling in love.
Looking every
eyes.
Hoping for the
first to drop her
for. We know
we won't find
anyone else
like us.
Us next to
nothing. Between
Baileys & nothing
I take Baileys.

the dimming light
reflecting glass in
the candle.
We are the only
inhabitants in
the room.
I believe you're
the only woman
who can keep me
safe. A sparrow
is all I can see
from the corner
of my eye.
I fit the battle
you hit the bottle.
I wasted my time.
enough to not
kill time with you.
Fill it like few.
How can you
sleep so happily?
When I'm seeing
Jupiter Swinging
low beneath
my eyes.
Your waxen
skin
desert dry.

I don't like
controlling your
high tide.
So I'm not
even gonna try.
Ain't gonna stop.
until I take
your hand.
I purpled your
eye lids. I tanned your skin
you never looked
so beautiful to
me. Does my
mind transform
your face. or do
your moods, to
such degree.
Middle age bloat
to swan float.
Shadows leak from you. I hear
every breath magni-
fied, the Chinese
dragon burns his lord.
You reach the top
of the world & watch
lives burn. Memories
staining the furniture,
dry mouths smile

their
sweetest.
Pale African redhead,
he'll comfort you.

September 1998

1

Take the glass, the third one, everything
is yours. What has satisfied? Come
on, even the gypsy doesn't know.
But the gypsy don't know nothing,
except spells about unsold roses.
And you try. I know. It makes you
cynically the Cyclops weird chick in
the message song, you ain't nothin'
but a . . .

You are everything, delicate, fragile,
feminine, truly the most. Our repetitions,
I listen & find faults. You don't even
want to hear.

Do we want only our pasts?
Those pasts, which are people, here,
right now to add what is needed?
We want privacy. But where are
the invaders who want to know what
shouldn't happen will be seen by them?

2

There was temporary perfection.

It was after separation. My
private knowledge. Avoided judgment.

The best ones know. The last bones
towed and buried. Just pretend I never
bothered you.

February 1999

I miss the sex, all its aspects.
All my respects.
The kink started to make it sink
                              For me.
To have your face in someone's
crotch with your mouth full of booze
and someone's finger up
your ass
and ten minutes later
sitting in a cab like nothing,
legs crossed, hands in lap.

But the perfect interlocking
of our necks, and her tongue
on my neck, the constant
warmth of her poreless
skin that can never be revived.

October 1998

Well I ain't gonna
tell you no story,
I ain't gonna tell you
no lie, I'm not gonna
make the slightest effort.
You who have fallen
in laps, needy laps.
Oh, how great that there was
nothing to prove.
Oil & vinegar don't mix.
We mix.
Like the lion and
the sand, the moon
& the spoon. Like the
Fire & the coal, like
the crack and the pipe,
the hopeful dope, the hateful
mother, shadows &
                    surface.
          My Japanese wisp.

December 1998

Tin rain
hornblower
shark suit blowjobber
or bob her head
around the world
She left her dying turtles
hid her rolling bottles
bid her other troubles
to a bar full of doubles,
on the rocks.
Sharing shocks
elect a cut
in bargain basement

August 1998

730 DAYS

1

This same position
of our last day.
      That I'm photographed in,
that I drew myself in.
      The mess that was
packed up,
      has exploded again.
      My back was turned
and pensive in Japanese
characters. And in
character.
      The charcoal smudge
of your mood. The
crumbs of your mistrust
that I would eat off the floor, after
a sick sleep, for lunch
in the evening.
      Your acknowledgment
meant nothing. It
wouldn't slide by <u>my</u> pride.

2

I called you the morn-
ing before. Re-borning in
a tub of iron ore. In a

womb of wounded birds,
you got me wrapped in a
towel, me in my midtown
muddle, you took the
uptown tunnel, underneath
         bridging fantasies.
I'll just say pink
and gleaming. Down
on the ground. Downy,
it floated down,
we brushed them off
the bed. It <u>was</u>
the morning after.
The mourning began
the evening, black.
It was conspired.
And black my soul
attired. And gray
our souls, after walking
through dust of fires.

         3
long separation,
         early dawn aspiration.
Begin the cancellation

         4
End the cancellation.
End the celebration

of pain through
emotional ground-
breaking that
tells me I'm alive.

5
With my weight
lifted, and my weight loss.
        Blur and Mime
and what was there
to get through?

Why weren't they there,
Why weren't you there?

        And I laughed when
        <u>you</u> cried, the only
        one who made <u>me</u>
        cry not shamelessly
        but pridelessly.

And I had given
up on those situations
and your weakness
and my tightness.

6
Oh god it
was too good.

Love me, I think
you never stopped
I think I had to
look back and know
that every moment
of honesty, at her
expense, God save me,
goes down to your flesh
and forgivefulness.
And faith in the
face of all. And our
  doom to spend
  the dawns together.
In Love.

October 1997

If I could get
out what I feel
for everyone, it would
be a violent Love.
I would crack ribs
bite off lips
swallow tongues
and scratch my name
across your heart.

December 1997

1

Bob Dylan said
someone showed me
a picture of Dignity.
I just had to laugh,
dignity's never been photographed.
Dignity to let yourself
be knocked down, robbed,
Insulted, let paranoid
Gangsters take hold & try
to prevent for the safety of a
friend. Dignity is putting on the
Mask of Dignity & then taking
it off & let be seen in the eyes
In Mexico Masks and Mascaras
meaning more faces. Or more
layers & personalities without
Freudian shit stuck to your
shoes & stinking up the place.
Dignity is no compromise.
Dragging yourself bloated, half
dead to make 20,000
people's wish come true.
To know that much worse

has happened to better men,
for a reason, only the strongest
soul can take the pain. In
all its Forms.
Dignity is no complaint.
Not feeling guilt over
money or position.
Hurt yourself to cover
up happiness. Which
automatically leads to sadness,
Melancholy. But if you
can love man or woman,
for one out of 365 days
you got it made.
Let that memory lift
you.
Not putting every one against
a wall by them knowing
you don't get what you
want, you'll find some other
little way to do it.
Dignity is no Fight. Having
such greatness that everything
is forgiven.
Yes, dignity is not throwing
your trash unless you
want manslaughter from
a slipped banana peel &

a broken neck.
Dignity is feeling happy
that friends & family
are coming.
Though I shall be accused
of everything but dignity.
But I love to see them happy.
Her laughter on the phone.
Dignity of Whores at least
when treated like queens
they are.
Proud of Family, her Five
Children from the same
amount of fathers.
In one room Damp as
a greasy pan cleaning sponge.
Happy with photo albums. Her
oldest boy w/ one eye crossed.
Felt no shame or hurt,
or anything to hide.
The Queen of Spain who
when I asked her where
should I spit out my gum
which I was holding
inches from her face said
in Spanish accented English
"Just on the grass."
Not taking insult &

criticism as the others
lack of understanding.
Unless it's often they talked to you.

A 23 year old Punk Kid—
T-Bone—who takes a
bus from Florida to Prov.
R.I. to get a blow job &
then beaten to shit by his
best friends for some little
Movie. He stepped up fine,
with a brick gash on his
head & went on a drinking
binge carrying a jug of Jim Beam.

Humility Vs. Arrogance

Keeping Dignity in hard situations
means the killing off
of
High & low,
Apathy arrives.
Does a good job for a while,
then extremes are needed.
Then you come cheap &
see, hear, feel the dignity of
the morning, laundry being washed,
roosters crowing, Trash Truck

rumbles, hear yells, Fresh
fruit squeezed. The End of
Silence & smooth nerves.
Just the harmless
beginning of an angry
hatefilled, Rape filled,
Child beating, dog
kicking, gunshooting,
knifestabbing,
Bled to death day.

I believe in Jesus
I believe in Elvis
believe in whiskey
in love and hate
pot
my faded jeans
your dress
broad pink stripes
thin black ones
your troubled black face
her growing hair and moon glasses
glass shadows and goldness
music work music play
turned up and down
dying living
sweating out laughing out
roses on your pockets
thin black mustached
five spot monastery
not shown up
and shown up tight
the short circuit
matches lighting
knocking your ear
trying to block my road

my mind block ock
sindental
going out of your way
to not get along
your light skull
forehead
chicks got nice legs
like you'd say it
the repetition
of my symbolism
talks back to me
in a Oaxaca
whorehouse smelling
jasmine
lost around alone the corner
with just her name
countdown to death
10 9 8 7
sixties sharpness
sharkskin shoes
her slapped ass
thin tits
your life is a
shock therapy
300 an hour
mine is numb therapy
poundin' head
intellectualize or

institutionalize
16 white Cadillacs.
An orange Gravitron
believes in me

HURRICANE

1

I ain't gonna write no odes.
I'll get asphalt, build new roads.
You gotta tell me the color of
your eyes. And, if they're dark
eyes, I won't throw you out
and take your glory.
Though ugliest woman has her
beauty, hairline, toe nails,
Fuck my magnifier, let Bob
Dylan find his commies.
It was beautiful, you trying
to get to sleep with your
head on my lap. A woman
hadn't touched me affectionately
in months, until you put
your hands through my hair.
No obsession, or fanati-
cism, just precious
             fact.
Your life shall be the
             best.

2

The passing of notes,
which take everything back

to childhood, no jadedness.
The only true unconditional love,
and remember, each man kills
the thing he loves. Don't fight
your death, show you know it.
Don't rebel, (this could go on)
you should revel, reveal, with
velocity, with veracity, exact-
itude, verisimilitude, lovelihood
(does the word exist?), Resist no
censorship. Towards you. Towards
others.
                (This is all shit,
                Only one word comes)
                        Lovers.

        3
The most unfortunate things,
Worst karmic Luck can't get me
down. Why your smile? 'Cause I
might not see it again. I'll live
with shit forever. Dried on the
sole of my shoe. "But if the
shoe fits, wear it." They say (the tacky
fuckers) next time I try harder
to squeeze into your platform boots.
And I know you don't need white
wings to fly. But I do need an angel
to help me soar.

Someone to do my things
for. Not audiences. I never
want to hear a critic.
I want to hear you that my
painting is alive, full of a new
form of expression. I
want to hear your words which
you called "cursi" which have
open emotion, that
scares, calculating hard boiled
people.
I want to trust people, I want
to stop my games. Somehow you
saw that's what I was being.
Not somehow, you did.

Hardboiled nut
Plywood soul
quickly emptying
bleary hearted
nothing but destruction
if eyes are windows
to the soul, my soul
is bloodshot
my voice might comfort
when it's full of coke
I got while I
deserved it
and loved it
which couldn't hang on
and I love you for
teaching me to love and kill

June 1993

Great ocean, always equal,
always yourself.
Who judges you by your
weakest ripple or most destructive
wave?
The king inside him does
Water of oceans that can't be
drunk. Water that currently
makes the king lose his bearings.
      Ocean where loners unknown to
      you save your gasping body
      beyond the reef, "That forgotten
man who ended my greatest
decision ever, of suicide!"

Oceanfront where utopian sex happens.
Whether sun up down,
          crash or skim.
      You can enter like a conqueror or
a seducer.
      <u>Be</u> seduced, be warned.
His wet towels will have to be
picked up by someone.
      Dry ones, you can't take
          your time.

February 1999

TEXASS / TEXIS

Black plum Nightingales
know how to move

Dry White crackers
get pecked on

Is your ass Tex or Mex
or black or White?
or is it gone numb
and nowhere?

1996

I know that something
Repels her.
I don't want to go into
Medical/Physical drawback
lists. This is not self pity.
I can sometimes see it in her
eyes when I come out of the
bathroom
but it's good she wasn't
afraid to slap me, punch me
bite me.
That makes her worthwhile
and me conditionally uncon-
ditional.

November 1998

Oh the poor body,
        that's been battered.
That is now differently
      afraid.

      Caution is cared to
I'm caring more sitting
on the bathroom floor
that the storm let us
stay in. Guided by green
street light lamp 10,000 feet
above, in a time before
radio communication.

But baby's wails come clear
at the "Fiesta Inn."
Where the siesta is
being enforced at 5 A.M.

We needed, we need
that bubble life.
Strangers can feel comfort in it
and the Jacuzzi.
We were twins,
we were transplanted sins.

Who's the gentle man?
Who makes the other stay.
Aging & refreshing.
Really naked under the stars.
Pleasing, I hope, went far.
The Occident and Orient.
Tan you deep. Leave your
pale feet. Rhythming
speech. My Dominican.
Via France, and Arab
steel. I will
                    never
                    grab & force.
'Cause you're the
            One I never forget.

February 1999

Personalizing physical pain
Physicalizing personal pain
Tell me make a fiction of this
Tell 'em that is where we'll
Spend the rest of our lives
Strumming bum hum tune
Why do I need your fire
When I can project it on a screen

Who's gonna need your life
When your life works
Are collected leatherbound
And you're nothin' but a hound

Melancholics Anonymous join us
down the line in the sad savannahs.
When my worst jokes and self ruin
fantasies come to life.
For once I'm up against the wall,
thumbtacked & humpbacked,
misshapen, mistaken
and taken in.
Even the loneliest woman can turn
you into a one night stand.
Get caught breakin' in, your fresh heart
in my hand.

December 1997

1

Whiskey Sour
My medicine sours
Got no more understandin' of this body
Week of sacrifice, body dripping
Weak of faith or fate

Old Granddad, dead on the rocks,
Dancing Flirting
Smiling with everyone
Wolf is dead and
Melon is singing
Sweating and whitehaired

The ice melting Paleolithic
The girl wiping his sweat
Is trying to get in touch
With his brownness
We're all God's children

2

Her ghostliness and freedom;
I don't understand bar maid shout
And only junk mind

Turning into pure child
Rejuvenation

Her stories come to bed with me
Worries come out my body
Out of lots of bodies
Just angry
'Cause there's nothin' can be done
But hope for a 99 life cat
Flat on feet

1

Dylan Thomas,
now, I can only
watch you now,
knowing it's not
your name.
Knowing it's
no good making
repetitions.
I simply watch
you sleeping.

2

In my wakefulness
helped by four stran-
gers. And really
no urge for
contact because
of my coke
sweat, at 11 A.M.
when I imagine
much more from
your orange-brown
leather jacket.

3

And my two
last sips
of tequila,
now watered
down to last
a little longer.
Now still not
finished. Your
over scratching
feet, pulling down
covers.

4

Putting down
legs. Last night's
dreams of
general overall
controller. I
look up, looking
for inspiration
and seeing
leather jacket

5

turned into
goat face
and twisted

alligator head.
Your loveless
friends made
us seem, made
it seem to
me like we

6
were the only
ones happy
to touch each-
other. Period.
    I
                want
                    on.

September 1998

clingon rusty spoon
use you like a bottle cap
rush you into the bathroom
rush me into the heart boom
doomed & sizzled
      frayed hangover
take the freight train
to great place.

August 1998

The ganas left me
　　　　for my world
　　　　　　　this life
　　　　which is 20 years
　　　　　　　of destruction,
　　　　　　　of bad seeds,
　　　　everything to drive you crazy
people scared to death of uselessness
　　　　which is all there is
　　　　apart from the moment
　　　　you can help someone

　　　　I don't want to keep livin' it
　　　　like that
　　　　though I will and I can't
　　　　and don't
　　　　and I want

1993

You took me out of all of this. Because no delirium deforms you. But delirium does not deform a Van Gogh painting either. Vincent is the certainty that the sun will come out again. He is the certitude of moon and stars. Scientific truth does not exclude beauty. Indeed, it almost insists that we knock at its door. The placebos of joy and comfort are only added ingredients. They walk alone. They are not you. They are roots rotting in the kitchens of vanity, never of divinity. And yet we go on repeating it all, over and over.

Look: I am opening up all the avenues of my sensations. If I keep them canned, they will wound my living flesh. My humors must be fixed in the deepest and most oppressed color purple.

Look: is there a love more tender than this simple being there?

She reacted the way I knew she would. She judged. She condemned the mind to inexistence. The flowers we searchingly yearned for were pressed under the bathroom door. I interrupted. And told the truth and began to cry. I could only stammer that I could never, I never could, live without her.

But right here, who knows anything about love? I softly rest my hand on hers. I become excited. Then, for a few minutes, I am alone. Or stop in the landing, outside her apartment. I simply try to hide as much as I can. Nothing, no connection with connections, with the exhibited, with the thought of. I only want everyone off the bus: our sentiments are not visible to the rest of the passengers. We cover them up with the very practical anorak . . .

Love: your printed word is a hard, cold rock. But when you are not there, it grows. I try to touch you and you vanish.

Damned, beautiful woman, exhausted by jubilation. With time, gravity takes over. I embrace you near the outer patio. There I kiss you. Your truthful, mestizo blood possesses all the elements, it is persistent, mineral blood. It won't let me think that we will last forever.

We are in the back seat of the car, our eyes closed, our fingertips discovering the exact place.

May 5, 1999

SON OF SPERANZA

At his feet of silvery black
Or the pillar of pink, elevating joy
He charms the blossoming lilies at night
Collects suspicious wolves at dawn
aesthetic Orpheus, he charms, charms;
Delicate, hating and shocked alike.

A musical voice in a soft Hercules
He dreams of a flower, a flower of sun
Caressed by silken, lavender hands.

1986

Will I live tomorrow, just
          can't say. But I ain't goin'
away. This room is my nucleus.
To think huddled under a blanket is
escape, eyes closed hearing my fear
that's hidden in the silence, that
when broken is evil & unknown.
Unknown is welcome, but my reaction
which will be unknown frightens.
Except when it really is unexpected.
Then my paranoia doesn't have time
to think the worst and the beauty
arrives full force. The predictable doesn't
exist, which is its most frightening aspect.

My hidden things, not out of fright
but of not wanting to deal with
half-thinking brains' ignorances,
liberate. I want to see you
in the same position, you'd be
rocking yourself in tears, and your
weak surrounders won't be around in
another week.

          Each man kills the thing he
loves. Each woman lets herself

be loved to death. <u>Which</u> is dying
to love? Liquid tortures, but your
mouth is always wet though your
lips are sometimes dry. Mine are
sometimes swollen contagious kisses.
So were theirs and I didn't care,
I knew & ignored they didn't care
in the best or worst. The sheep as
lamb. The mother as whore: a tutor
to her own.

Is that what it seemed, wandering
in seeminess? A woman 30 a
girl 11. Pink mini skirts, heels (I
don't remember color), silver (I hope)
tank tops, swinging patent leather
purses, hair pulled back, bangs.
They were on the same corner, yes in
Juarez, but it was almost my
birthday, no Easter eggs, nothing
hidden, everything easy to find.

September 1998

I met Carlos Fuentes Lemus in 1976, while his father served as Mexican ambassador to France. He was about four years old, and we all called him Carlitos. I remember that he and his sister Natasha looked at me with curiosity and admiration. Carlos Fuentes had referred to me as the author of *Juan the Landless* and Juan the Landless was the hero in one of their comic books.

Later, I saw him with his parents when he was a teenager—with that look of innocence and eternal youth that he retained until his death—in Paris, New York, and, in May 1989, in Berlin. I was there for a few weeks on a grant from the DAAD, and he took a Polaroid of my friend Zeyni and me, which hangs on the wall of my office where I write these lines. Carlos Fuentes Lemus was a guarded, shy, introverted young man, who was endowed with a boundless curiosity: he enjoyed our strolls in the Turkish neighborhood of Kreuzberg, and seemed awestruck by the sight of the Wall and its insurmountable perimeter of wire fences and watchtowers. None of us could imagine that this menacing and apparently immutable backdrop was about to be taken apart and swept away by the "phantom of liberty."

But my friendship with him was forged much later. In

1992 we saw each other during the summer workshops in Spain at the Escorial: there he expressed his desire to travel to Morocco. I invited him to visit me at my home in Marrakech. He arrived a few months later, a day before his sister Natasha came from London. They stayed for a week. I knew from his father about the illness that consumed him, that he endured with an unassailable outer serenity. Nonetheless, I sensed his vulnerability, and the terrible burden that he carried awakened in those of us around him a desire to protect him from himself and from others. He spoke to me in that characteristic Spanish of his, of one who doesn't feel at home in the language he steps into, but who is a furtive visitor. One night—the hours he kept were different from mine—after mustering up the courage with the help of a swig from his flask of whiskey, he let me read twenty of his poems written in English. I knew about his incursions into the field of film (as well as his talent as a photographer) but I had no idea that he was a poet. I remember that I spent hours captivated by lines that revealed what I sensed: beautiful, startling lines, without the least self-complacency, imbued with a hidden and unsettling pain. I have always been enchanted by the magic of English poetry, and its ability to express more in fewer words than can other languages that I know. Carlos Fuentes Lemus moved within its sphere almost on tiptoe, oblivious to any rhetoric and easy sentimentalism, with the delicacy and weightlessness with which he fleetingly traced his path through life.

His poems about death are perhaps the most poignant

precisely because of the economy of emotion in his words: the unresigned acceptance of life as a fortuitous and temporary gift. "The *ganas* left me / for my world," admits the poet, and, before the undeserved severity of the punishment imposed on innocence, he foresees—without betraying emotion—his solitary descent into nothingness, when

> No more rays of orange sun
> Or streaks of reddening white
> They all shall glide into the past,
> I shall land into the future.

His early intuition about his destiny is accompanied by a generosity and an ethical rigor that characterize all the writing of Carlos Fuentes Lemus: Dignity is "To know that much worse / has happened to better men." In writing about the "open emotion, that / scares, calculating hardboiled / people," the poet evokes the splendor of the present moment: a series of images of bodies that come together, he says, in search of a "conditionally unconditional" surrender.

The homage Carlos Fuentes Lemus pays to writers and artists and his sharp and demystifying portraits of major metropolises reveal his verbal ability to synthesize complex situations, as F. Scott Fitzgerald would say, "to hold two opposed ideas in the mind at the same time, and still retain the ability to function." After reading the poems of Carlos Fuentes Lemus, I recall the lines that Luis Cernuda wrote at the time of Lorca's death:

"Poets, like gods, reclaim only / the insubstantial part of life."
An insubstantiality that centers in an enduring way around
the memory of one who knew how to illuminate the beauty
and precision of words in his mad race against time.

JUAN GOYTISOLO
Translated by Alejandro Branger

EDITOR'S NOTE

I visited Carlos Fuentes Lemus at his family's home in Mexico City during my Spring break, in 1999, to help restructure his unfinished movie, *Gallo de Pelea*. There we recorded many hours of Fuentes Lemus reading some of the fifty poems that he considered for the film's soundscape. I had been asked to serve as guest creative writing editor for *the minnesota review*, and I solicited several of Fuentes Lemus's poems for the issue. He was overjoyed until he saw me smiling, at which point he suppressed all but a smile. This was to be his first poetry publication, and he talked about putting together a book.

When he died, less than two months later, his parents asked me to return to Mexico City. Alejandro Branger was there too. In that time of sorrow, the two of us kept busy trying to put Fuentes Lemus's papers in order. We gathered a film script (about Elvis Presley in his late years), a film outline (*Gallo*), watercolor storyboards (for an adaptation of his father's book *Aura*), sketches in pen, photographs, and hundreds of poems and parts of poems written on manual typewriter and by uneven hand on small scraps of paper or large sheets of drawing stock, all left higgledy-piggledy around his crowded bedroom. Often the poems had stanza numbers, which led me to believe many were incomplete or partially lost. Many included the dates and times of their completion. Later his parents found more poems in London. Often Fuentes Lemus had left poems wherever in the world he had written them, as scattered as his friendships, and his friends sent in others still. For instance, his girlfriend sent the prose poem he wrote the day he died. Eventually the word-processed and printed stack of poems was about three-and-a-half-inches thick, including some almost identical versions and instances in which one poem had been "folded" into another. There were enough poems for a book, and the family, representing his estate, accepted my proposal that I edit them.

Much of this selection consists of poems that appeared to be Fuentes Lemus's favorites judging from the fact that he had committed them to tape. The choice of poems represents his most constant obsessions and concerns, and also includes some of his earliest work in order to show, despite stylistic change, the continuity in his thought. The order of the poems reflects some of Fuentes Lemus and my late-night discussions about the progress of his life. For this book I've retained certain idiosyncrasies (variant spellings, absent hyphens, underlining and lack of italics, and compound or other words split in two) to give a reader the astonishing feeling I had of reading the manuscripts as a new and uncharted territory.

INDEX OF FIRST LINES

CARLOS FUENTES LEMUS, son of Mexican writer Carlos Fuentes and journalist Silvia Lemus, was a writer, photographer, painter, and director. A life-long hemophiliac, he died at the age of twenty-five in Puerto Vallarta.

E. SHASKAN BUMAS wrote the story collection *The Price of Tea in China*, which was a finalist for PEN America West Fiction Book of the Year. He teaches at New Jersey City University.

Petros Abatzoglou, *What Does Mrs. Freeman Want?*
Michal Ajvaz, *The Golden Age.*
  The Other City.
Pierre Albert-Birot, *Grabinoulor.*
Yuz Aleshkovsky, *Kangaroo.*
Felipe Alfau, *Chromos.*
  Locos.
João Almino, *The Book of Emotions.*
Ivan Ângelo, *The Celebration.*
  The Tower of Glass.
David Antin, *Talking.*
António Lobo Antunes, *Knowledge of Hell.*
  The Splendor of Portugal.
Alain Arias-Misson, *Theatre of Incest.*
Iftikhar Arif and Waqas Khwaja, eds., *Modern Poetry of Pakistan.*
John Ashbery and James Schuyler, *A Nest of Ninnies.*
Robert Ashley, *Perfect Lives.*
Gabriela Avigur-Rotem, *Heatwave and Crazy Birds.*
Heimrad Bäcker, *transcript.*
Djuna Barnes, *Ladies Almanack.*
  Ryder.
John Barth, *LETTERS.*
  Sabbatical.
Donald Barthelme, *The King.*
  Paradise.
Svetislav Basara, *Chinese Letter.*
René Belletto, *Dying.*
Mark Binelli, *Sacco and Vanzetti Must Die!*
Andrei Bitov, *Pushkin House.*
Andrej Blatnik, *You Do Understand.*
Louis Paul Boon, *Chapel Road.*
  My Little War.
  Summer in Termuren.
Roger Boylan, *Killoyle.*
Ignácio de Loyola Brandão, *Anonymous Celebrity.*
  The Good-Bye Angel.
  Teeth under the Sun.
  Zero.
Bonnie Bremser, *Troia: Mexican Memoirs.*
Christine Brooke-Rose, *Amalgamemnon.*
Brigid Brophy, *In Transit.*
Meredith Brosnan, *Mr. Dynamite.*
Gerald L. Bruns, *Modern Poetry and the Idea of Language.*
Evgeny Bunimovich and J. Kates, eds., *Contemporary Russian Poetry: An Anthology.*
Gabrielle Burton, *Heartbreak Hotel.*
Michel Butor, *Degrees.*
  Mobile.
  Portrait of the Artist as a Young Ape.
G. Cabrera Infante, *Infante's Inferno.*
  Three Trapped Tigers.
Julieta Campos, *The Fear of Losing Eurydice.*
Anne Carson, *Eros the Bittersweet.*
Orly Castel-Bloom, *Dolly City.*
Camilo José Cela, *Christ versus Arizona.*
  The Family of Pascual Duarte.
  The Hive.
Louis-Ferdinand Céline, *Castle to Castle.*
  Conversations with Professor Y.
  London Bridge.

  Normance.
  North.
  Rigadoon.
Hugo Charteris, *The Tide Is Right.*
Jerome Charyn, *The Tar Baby.*
Eric Chevillard, *Demolishing Nisard.*
Marc Cholodenko, *Mordechai Schamz.*
Joshua Cohen, *Witz.*
Emily Holmes Coleman, *The Shutter of Snow.*
Robert Coover, *A Night at the Movies.*
Stanley Crawford, *Log of the S.S. The Mrs Unguentine.*
  Some Instructions to My Wife.
Robert Creeley, *Collected Prose.*
René Crevel, *Putting My Foot in It.*
Ralph Cusack, *Cadenza.*
Susan Daitch, *L.C.*
  Storytown.
Nicholas Delbanco, *The Count of Concord.*
  Sherbrookes.
Nigel Dennis, *Cards of Identity.*
Peter Dimock, *A Short Rhetoric for Leaving the Family.*
Ariel Dorfman, *Konfidenz.*
Coleman Dowell, *The Houses of Children.*
  Island People.
  Too Much Flesh and Jabez.
Arkadii Dragomoshchenko, *Dust.*
Rikki Ducornet, *The Complete Butcher's Tales.*
  The Fountains of Neptune.
  The Jade Cabinet.
  The One Marvelous Thing.
  Phosphor in Dreamland.
  The Stain.
  The Word "Desire."
William Eastlake, *The Bamboo Bed.*
  Castle Keep.
  Lyric of the Circle Heart.
Jean Echenoz, *Chopin's Move.*
Stanley Elkin, *A Bad Man.*
  Boswell: A Modern Comedy.
  Criers and Kibitzers, Kibitzers and Criers.
  The Dick Gibson Show.
  The Franchiser.
  George Mills.
  The Living End.
  The MacGuffin.
  The Magic Kingdom.
  Mrs. Ted Bliss.
  The Rabbi of Lud.
  Van Gogh's Room at Arles.
François Emmanuel, *Invitation to a Voyage.*
Annie Ernaux, *Cleaned Out.*
Lauren Fairbanks, *Muzzle Thyself.*
  Sister Carrie.
Leslie A. Fiedler, *Love and Death in the American Novel.*
Juan Filloy, *Op Oloop.*
Gustave Flaubert, *Bouvard and Pécuchet.*
Kass Fleisher, *Talking out of School.*
Ford Madox Ford, *The March of Literature.*
Jon Fosse, *Aliss at the Fire.*
  Melancholy.
Max Frisch, *I'm Not Stiller.*

FOR A FULL LIST OF PUBLICATIONS, VISIT:
www.dalkeyarchive.com

Man in the Holocene.
CARLOS FUENTES, *Christopher Unborn.*
Distant Relations.
Terra Nostra.
Where the Air Is Clear.
WILLIAM GADDIS, *J R.*
The Recognitions.
JANICE GALLOWAY, *Foreign Parts.*
The Trick Is to Keep Breathing.
WILLIAM H. GASS, *Cartesian Sonata
and Other Novellas.*
Finding a Form.
A Temple of Texts.
The Tunnel.
Willie Masters' Lonesome Wife.
GÉRARD GAVARRY, *Hoppla! 1 2 3.*
Making a Novel.
ETIENNE GILSON,
The Arts of the Beautiful.
Forms and Substances in the Arts.
C. S. GISCOMBE, *Giscome Road.*
Here.
Prairie Style.
DOUGLAS GLOVER, *Bad News of the Heart.*
The Enamoured Knight.
WITOLD GOMBROWICZ,
A Kind of Testament.
KAREN ELIZABETH GORDON,
The Red Shoes.
GEORGI GOSPODINOV, *Natural Novel.*
JUAN GOYTISOLO, *Count Julian.*
Exiled from Almost Everywhere.
Juan the Landless.
Makbara.
Marks of Identity.
PATRICK GRAINVILLE, *The Cave of Heaven.*
HENRY GREEN, *Back.*
Blindness.
Concluding.
Doting.
Nothing.
JACK GREEN, *Fire the Bastards!*
JIŘÍ GRUŠA, *The Questionnaire.*
GABRIEL GUDDING,
Rhode Island Notebook.
MELA HARTWIG, *Am I a Redundant
Human Being?*
JOHN HAWKES, *The Passion Artist.*
Whistlejacket.
ALEKSANDAR HEMON, ED.,
Best European Fiction.
AIDAN HIGGINS, *A Bestiary.*
Balcony of Europe.
Bornholm Night-Ferry.
Darkling Plain: Texts for the Air.
Flotsam and Jetsam.
Langrishe, Go Down.
Scenes from a Receding Past.
Windy Arbours.
KEIZO HINO, *Isle of Dreams.*
KAZUSHI HOSAKA, *Plainsong.*
ALDOUS HUXLEY, *Antic Hay.*
Crome Yellow.
Point Counter Point.
Those Barren Leaves.
Time Must Have a Stop.
NAOYUKI II, *The Shadow of a Blue Cat.*
MIKHAIL IOSSEL AND JEFF PARKER, EDS.,
*Amerika: Russian Writers View the
United States.*
DRAGO JANČAR, *The Galley Slave.*
GERT JONKE, *The Distant Sound.*

Geometric Regional Novel.
Homage to Czerny.
The System of Vienna.
JACQUES JOUET, *Mountain R.*
Savage.
Upstaged.
CHARLES JULIET, *Conversations with
Samuel Beckett and Bram van
Velde.*
MIEKO KANAI, *The Word Book.*
YORAM KANIUK, *Life on Sandpaper.*
HUGH KENNER, *The Counterfeiters.*
*Flaubert, Joyce and Beckett:
The Stoic Comedians.*
Joyce's Voices.
DANILO KIŠ, *Garden, Ashes.*
A Tomb for Boris Davidovich.
ANITA KONKKA, *A Fool's Paradise.*
GEORGE KONRÁD, *The City Builder.*
TADEUSZ KONWICKI, *A Minor Apocalypse.*
The Polish Complex.
MENIS KOUMANDAREAS, *Koula.*
ELAINE KRAF, *The Princess of 72nd Street.*
JIM KRUSOE, *Iceland.*
EWA KURYLUK, *Century 21.*
EMILIO LASCANO TEGUI, *On Elegance
While Sleeping.*
ERIC LAURRENT, *Do Not Touch.*
HERVÉ LE TELLIER, *The Sextine Chapel.*
*A Thousand Pearls (for a Thousand
Pennies)*
VIOLETTE LEDUC, *La Bâtarde.*
EDOUARD LEVÉ, *Autoportrait.*
Suicide.
SUZANNE JILL LEVINE, *The Subversive
Scribe: Translating Latin
American Fiction.*
DEBORAH LEVY, *Billy and Girl.*
*Pillow Talk in Europe and Other
Places.*
JOSÉ LEZAMA LIMA, *Paradiso.*
ROSA LIKSOM, *Dark Paradise.*
OSMAN LINS, *Avalovara.*
The Queen of the Prisons of Greece.
ALF MAC LOCHLAINN,
The Corpus in the Library.
Out of Focus.
RON LOEWINSOHN, *Magnetic Field(s).*
MINA LOY, *Stories and Essays of Mina Loy.*
BRIAN LYNCH, *The Winner of Sorrow.*
D. KEITH MANO, *Take Five.*
MICHELINE AHARONIAN MARCOM,
The Mirror in the Well.
BEN MARCUS,
The Age of Wire and String.
WALLACE MARKFIELD,
Teitlebaum's Window.
To an Early Grave.
DAVID MARKSON, *Reader's Block.*
Springer's Progress.
Wittgenstein's Mistress.
CAROLE MASO, *AVA.*
LADISLAV MATEJKA AND KRYSTYNA
POMORSKA, EDS.,
*Readings in Russian Poetics:
Formalist and Structuralist Views.*
HARRY MATHEWS,
*The Case of the Persevering Maltese:
Collected Essays.*
Cigarettes.
The Conversions.
The Human Country: New and